BIBLE EXPL

Devised by an ecumenica
the Baptist Union o
the Church of
the Methodist and United Reformed
the National Christian Education Council;
and Sheffield Christian Education Council.

Peter

This *Guidebook* is for the use of
Explorers and Leaders
and was written by **Revd Paul Martin**
**Minister of Leavesden Road Baptist Church, Watford and
Convenor of the Baptist Union Children's Working Group**

The ecumenical group responsible for *Bible Exploration* consists of:
Elizabeth Bruce, National Christian Education Council
Wendy Carolan, National Christian Education Council
Anne Dunkley, Baptist Union of Great Britain
Judy Jarvis, Methodist Church
Rosemary Johnston, United Reformed Church
Steve Pearce, Church of England
Valerie Stephens, Sheffield Christian Education Council

Abbreviations:
AV   Authorized Version

Published by:
National Christian Education Council
1020 Bristol Road
Selly Oak
Birmingham
B29 6LB

British Library Cataloguing in Publication Data:
A catalogue record for this book is available from the British Library.

ISBN 0-7197-0904-0

© 1997 National Christian Education Council

All rights reserved. No part of this publication may be
reproduced, stored in a retrieval system, or transmitted, in
any form or by any means, electronic, mechanical,
photocopied, recorded or otherwise, without the prior
permission of the Publisher.

Typeset by the National Christian Education Council.
Printed and bound in Great Britain.

CONTENTS

	Page
Syllabus	**4**
Introduction	**5**
Fisherman turns follower (Call)	**9**
Foundation stone to stumbling block (Declaration)	**15**
A sheep running scared... (Denial)	**25**
...to Shepherd of the flock (Restoration)	**31**
From Gospel for some to Gospel for all (Development)	**37**
Notes for Leaders	**46**
● **Groups**	**46**
● **Question Papers**	**48**

BIBLE EXPLORATION - Peter

	ORANGE	YELLOW	GREEN	BLUE	PURPLE	WHITE
Call	Luke 5.1-11	Luke 5.1-11	Luke 5.1-11	Luke 5.1-11	Luke 5.1-11 John 1.35-42	Luke 5.1-11 John 1.35-42
Declaration	Matthew 16.13-18	Matthew 16.13-18	Matthew 16.13-24	Matthew 16.13-24	Matthew 16.13-24 14.22-33	Matthew 16.13-24 14.22-33
Denial	Mark 14.1-2 14.27-31 14.66-72	Mark 14.1-2 14.27-31 14.66-72	Mark 14.1-2 14.27-42 14.66-72	Mark 14.1-2 14.27-42 14.66-72	Mark 14.1-2 14.27-42 14.66-72	Mark 14.1-2 14.27-42 14.66-72
Restoration	John 21.1-17	John 21.1-17	John 21.1-17	John 21.1-17	John 21.1-19	John 21.1-19
Development	Acts 11.5-10 11.18	Acts 11.5-10 11.18	Acts 11.1-18	Acts 11.1-18	Acts 11.1-18 15.6-11	Acts 11.1-18 15.6-11

INTRODUCTION

Purpose
The main purpose of Bible Exploration is to encourage study of the Bible and to discover its truth and relevance for today.

Resources
Books
J Drane, *Evangelism for a New Age* (Marshall Pickering, 1994) pp. 97-114
J Parr (Ed), *Sowers & Reapers: A Companion to the Four Gospels and Acts*
    (Bible Reading Fellowship, 1994)
Articles on Peter in dictionaries and encyclopedias of the Bible
Song
'Fishermen come and fish for men'
(*Baptist Praise and Worship*, no. 196)

Group work and preparation
Exploring and learning can be done by individuals or groups. Using different methods and activities as well as engaging the imagination of the Explorers will make for more effective learning.

Any version of the Bible may be used for general study, but direct biblical quotations in this Guidebook, in the Workbooks and in the Bible Exploration Question Papers are taken from the *Good News Bible*. There are many versions of the Bible available; among the best for older groups are the *New Revised Standard Version* and the *Revised English Bible*.

Aim
To explore incidents and experiences which shaped Peter's faith and character, reflecting on them in the light of our own experience as followers of Jesus.

General introduction (All groups)

Peter is one of the few characters in the New Testament about whom there are enough stories and information to allow you to feel that you can relate to him as a person. Each of the four gospels has accounts of Peter's distinctive place within the company of twelve disciples. Peter, as pioneering leader and missionary, dominates the opening chapters of Acts. He is also mentioned in Paul's letters, a fact which indicates his prominence in the Early Church.

It is not only the amount of information, but the particular quality of that information, which helps us to engage with a real personality. The memories of Peter may well be coloured by the fact that he was prominent among the first leaders of the early Christian Church, but he is never portrayed as a 'plastic saint'. He has real character. His humanity and vulnerability are honestly and openly exposed.

Furthermore, the time-span which is covered by the accounts of Peter in the gospels and in Acts allows us to trace the ups and downs of Peter's Christian formation as follower and leader. From a firebrand fisherman on the shores of Lake Galilee, he developed into a wise, bridge-building leader at the Council of Jerusalem (Acts 15 – the last mention of Peter in the book of Acts). Peter's story is not one of overnight success. His pathway to maturity in Christian discipleship is marked by false starts, stumbles and diversions.

Biographical notes

So what background information can we glean about Peter from the pages of the New Testament? Matthew and John disagree about the name of Peter's father. Matthew names him Jonah (Matthew 16.17), while the fourth gospel identifies him as John (John 1.42 and 21.15). Some have suggested that the Aramaic *bar-yona* of Matthew is not intended as a reference to his father, but instead means 'terrorist'. However, there is not a great deal of support for this interpretation, and we probably have to live with the contradiction.

Peter had at least one brother, Andrew, who also followed Jesus. John 1.44 tells us that they came from Bethsaida (literally, 'house of the fisher') which, it is thought, was situated east of the Jordan, near the point where the River Jordan flows into the northern end of the Sea of Galilee. Although Bethsaida may well have been a Jewish town, it was located in Gentile surroundings.

Both 'Simon' and 'Andrew' are Greek names. This suggests that the family was influenced by the Greek culture around it. It is highly likely that anyone brought up in Bethsaida would not only have spoken Greek, but would have been familiar with Greek culture. It is interesting to note that, when some Greeks approached Jesus in Jerusalem, they turned for help to Philip, whose home town was also Bethsaida (John 12.21). Although possibly bilingual and familiar with both Jewish and Greek cultures, it is altogether probable that Peter had no formal education. In Acts 4.13 Peter is described as uneducated.

At some point, Peter and Andrew moved from Bethsaida to Capernaum, on the north-western shores of the Sea of Galilee, where they worked as fishermen. Here they lived with Peter's wife and mother-in-law (Mark 1.29-31). Peter's wife is also mentioned by Paul in 1 Corinthians 9.5, where Paul indicates that she accompanied Peter on his travels as an apostle.

What's in a name?

Peter is known by four different names in the pages of the New Testament.

On just two occasions he is named Simeon, a popular Hebrew name among the Jews (Acts 15.14 and 2 Peter 1.1 (AV)). This could well have been Peter's 'original' Jewish name.

Much more common is the use of Simon. He was probably known by this Greek name around Bethsaida and Capernaum. It was not unusual for Jews living in a Greek-speaking environment to be given both a Hebrew and a Greek name.

Thirdly, we find Peter given the descriptive title, 'Kepha', which is an Aramaic word meaning 'stone' or 'rock'. (When the Aramaic word is transcribed into Greek it is sometimes supplied with a final 's' to make it a more comfortable sounding word in Greek: thus 'Kephas', often written as 'Cephas' in English translations.) This is how Paul most often refers to Peter (Galatians 1.18; 2.9ff.; 1 Corinthians 1.12; 3.22; 9.5).

Finally, 'Kepha' has been translated into the Greek word 'Petros', which also means 'stone'. This has become our name 'Peter'. This title or 'nickname' was given to Peter by Jesus, although the gospel writers do not agree at what point the name was given. John 1.42 places the naming at their first meeting; Mark 3.16 associates the name with the calling of the twelve; and Matthew 16.18 links the name with Peter's confession of Jesus as the Messiah. Paul uses Petros in only one place (Galatians 2.7-8), but it is commonly used in the gospels, normally coupled with Simon. Although we now think of Peter as a name, it is likely that it was not used as a name initially, but more as a descriptive title – Simon, the Rock. Names, after all, are not normally translated into another language. (It is not unlike the way in which 'Jesus, the Messiah', was translated into Greek as 'Jesus, the Christ', with 'Christ' eventually taking the form of a name rather than a title.)

Throughout these notes, whatever name is used in the biblical text, we will always use the name Peter.

First among equals

Peter occupied a unique position in the circle of twelve disciples. Although the lists of the twelve disciples vary in detail, what is common to all of them is that Peter is named first (Mark 3.16; Matthew 10.2; Luke 6.14; Acts 1.13). The disciples can even be known as 'Simon and his companions' (Mark 1.36).

Almost always, if there is someone to speak for the disciples, it is Peter who is given the role. In the story of the transfiguration it is Peter who proposes that they erect tents (Mark 9.5); when there is a question to be asked about forgiveness, it is Peter who poses it (Matthew 18.21); when the disciples want to know who the parables are for, again Peter's voice is heard (Luke 12.41); it is Peter who reminds Jesus what the disciples have given up to follow him (Mark 10.28); and it is Peter who protests about Jesus washing his feet (John 13.6-9).

There is a strong tradition in the Early Church that Peter was the first witness of the resurrection (1 Corinthians 15.5, supported by Luke 24.34). However, the actual event is not recorded in the gospels.

Yet, for all his prominence, Peter is not portrayed as someone who is head and shoulders above everyone else when it comes to following Jesus, but rather as someone who stands out as a representative of the rest. He may be the only one who jumps out of the boat to walk on the water, but he is also the one who finds himself sinking (Matthew 14.28-31). Peter keeps on revealing that he has hardly begun to grasp the significance of Jesus' ministry, and finds himself the butt of Jesus' exasperation. It is this all-too-human side of Peter which allows us to identify with him.

To do together

● *Try to build up a sense of the kind of person Peter was:*
What would his hands look like?
What would his face look like?
What could you tell from his voice and the way he spoke?
How does he see his future?
What are his hopes and dreams?
What are the dangers which face him?
How would his close friends describe him?
What does he value?
Who values him?
Who are his friends?
What is his lifestyle like?

● *If you met someone like Peter, what do you think would be your first impressions? Would you warm to him? Would you be defensive? Would you be able to relate to him?*

● *How do you think Peter would fit into your group? Would he be a welcome member? Would you feel comfortable with him?*

(Members of the group could work in pairs, taking one or two questions each.)

FISHERMAN TURNS FOLLOWER (CALL)

Luke 5.1-11 and John 1.35-42

When we read the story of the call of the first disciples in Mark 1.16-20, we are tempted to ask the question, 'Whatever made them leave their nets and follow?' At that point in the story Mark has told us very little about Jesus, and there is no evidence that Simon, Andrew, James and John have ever set eyes on him or heard of him. The whole thing seems a complete mystery, and, for Mark, that's probably what it's meant to be.

When Luke comes to tell the story, it is as if he wants to take away some of that mystery - although not all of it. He is aware of the question, and seems to want to give us some answers. He does this in two ways. Firstly, as we shall see, he adds significantly to the story which Mark tells. Secondly, he ensures that both the reader and the characters have been introduced to Jesus before he invites them to follow him. News about Jesus has already spread throughout the territory of Galilee (Luke 4.14). He has already been to Capernaum, and indeed to Peter's house, where he has healed Peter's mother-in-law (Luke 4.38-39). Finally, our passage begins with Jesus teaching the crowds from the boat, so that the four who respond to Jesus' summons have had the opportunity to hear Jesus speaking. Their decision to follow becomes somewhat more understandable, although no less radical.

In Mark, interestingly, all this takes place *after* the call of Peter (Mark 1.29-31; 3.7-9).

Luke 5.1-11 (All groups)

Verses 1-3

Luke sets the scene. It is morning beside Lake Gennesaret, with the fishermen washing their nets after being out on the lake through the night. Lake Gennesaret (also known in the New Testament as the Sea of Galilee and the Lake Tiberias) is an inland freshwater lake surrounded by hills and high mountains. It is about 21 kilometres long, north to south, 13 kilometres across at its widest, and lies some 213 metres below sea-level. It has a thriving fishing industry. Luke has already implied that Peter lives in Capernaum (4.31 ff.), which is on the north-west coast of the lake.

However, to begin with, the fishermen and the lake are incidental. The focus of attention is on Jesus, whose popularity has been rising. He finds himself overwhelmed by the crush of people eager to listen to him. Luke wants to emphasize that the words of Jesus are what attract people's attention: whether the 'eloquent words' in the synagogue in Nazareth (4.22), or the words of 'authority and power' in Capernaum's synagogue (4.36). The crowds are pressing in on him because they recognize his words as the 'word of God' (5.1). In this setting, Jesus takes advantage of one of the two boats pulled up onto the beach, and asks Peter to push out from the shore, so that he can use the boat as a makeshift platform. Peter, doubtless, is all too willing to be of service. Notice that Jesus follows the normal custom of a teacher at that time by sitting down, while his listeners stand.

Verse 4

Having finished teaching the crowd, Jesus now invites Peter to push out into deeper waters and to lower the nets.

Galilean fishing boats were open craft, about 6 to 9 metres in length. It is not at all clear from the passage how many people are involved in this particular fishing 'partnership'. Peter has others in the boat with him, and James and John, who have the second boat, are described as partners (verses 7 and 10). It seems that they share a small fishing business. Why Luke fails to mention Peter's brother, Andrew, is strange. It may be his economy of style.

As property-owning, self-employed business people, these fishermen would not have been at the bottom of the social scale. However, neither would they have been wealthy. It was precisely this group of people in the society of the time who were finding their economic stability threatened by high taxes. Many were feeling insecure and some were falling into debt. On top of this, the fishing industry was as unpredictable then as it is now. Fishermen could spend a whole night fishing with nothing to show for it.

Verse 5

Probably the last thing Peter and his colleagues want to do by now is to go fishing again. They are no doubt ready to go home to bed after a disappointing night. A note of weariness sounds through the words, 'we worked hard all night long and caught nothing.' Yet Jesus has begun to capture Peter's heart and mind. He has won Peter's respect and trust. Peter addresses him, 'Master,' (Greek *epistata*) a form of address which we find only in Luke. It implies a recognition of authority. It is difficult to tell exactly how much reluctance or scepticism is implied in Peter's acquiescence – 'All right... if you say so.' Whether expectantly or half-heartedly, Peter is saying, 'I'm doing this only because you're the one who's asking.' Once again it is the authoritative 'word' of Jesus which elicits a response (the Greek means literally 'at your word').

Verses 6-7

Peter and his friends let down their nets. These would be large drag nets, with the top supported by floats and the bottom weighted with sinkers. The nets were used like a sieve, often with a circle of boats closing in on one another or towards the shore. The drama of this incident is highlighted by the fact that one boat alone cannot cope with the enormous catch of fish. Peter and his companions need to call for help from James and John. Even then, the two boats are in danger of sinking once all of the fish are hauled on board.

Verse 8

Note how, at this significant moment in the unfolding drama, Luke subtly introduces the longer name 'Simon Peter'. Up to this point he has simply been called Simon.

Whatever Peter has seen in Jesus before this point, he now finds himself totally overwhelmed. One might think that his first reaction would be to wrap Jesus in a warm and enthusiastic embrace. But the moment is so intense and so profound for Peter that his mind is not on the huge catch of fish, but on the person before him who fills him with awe and with a deep sense of unworthiness. The reaction of falling on his knees, of addressing Jesus as 'Lord', and of facing up to his own deep inadequacies, all reveal that Peter experiences this moment as an encounter with God. His reaction to Jesus is reminiscent of Moses before the burning bush (Exodus 3) and of Isaiah in the temple (Isaiah 6). He responds as one who finds himself confronted by the holiness of God, and simply wants to crawl away into a corner.

To think and talk about:
The 'Wow' factor
- What do you think made Peter react the way he did in his encounter with Jesus? For example, was it the wonder of encountering a miracle-worker, or was it the threatening nearness of Jesus who entered his own world of fishing?
- What makes us retreat in awe of God? For example, is it because God is indescribably different, or because God identifies with us and comes near?

Verses 9-10

Peter's amazement is shared by those in the boat with him, and by his partners, James and John. However, Luke tells the story very much as if Peter is centre-stage and the others are merely 'extras' in the drama. There is no conversation between Jesus and these others.

Jesus goes on to address Peter directly. He firstly responds to Peter's awesome fear at finding himself in the presence of the Holy One: 'Do not be afraid.' By the way in which Jesus continues, these words do not only refer back to the past, they also offer assurance for the future into which Jesus is now leading Peter: 'from now on you will be catching men.' This sounds much more like a prediction than an invitation or challenge. Luke doesn't include the words 'Follow me' which appear in other gospel accounts. It is more as if Peter finds himself falling into line with Jesus' plans for him.

Just what are Jesus' plans for Peter? The invitation to 'catch men' is an invitation to Peter to turn his attention from fish to people, and to join Jesus as an active partner in his mission of love in the world. From the very beginning, it would appear, Jesus called people to him not just to follow and to learn from him, but also to be actively engaged with him in the tasks of the Kingdom.

The whole episode seems to say that when Jesus calls people to this task there is no reason to be afraid. If Jesus could help professional fishermen to catch fish beyond their wildest dreams, how much more will he guide and equip them in the task of drawing people into the net of the Kingdom of God? It comes across rather like an 'acted parable'.

Verse 11

The incident ends with the boats being dragged up onto the beach, and the fishermen leaving everything in order to become disciples of Jesus. If we take the story at face value, it means that they turn their backs on the best catch they have ever landed; that they leave behind their business; and that their family life will never be the same again. Jesus brings about a total change of priorities, and alters their life and lifestyle completely.

This readiness to be uprooted and travel the country, following a spiritual leader, can be set in the context of life in Palestine at that period. The whole region was in a state of social, economic, political and spiritual ferment. Many people were choosing to uproot themselves for a variety of reasons: some to emigrate; some to become political terrorists; some to join religious communities such as the one at Qumran... and some to follow Jesus. The time was ripe for people to take on an alternative lifestyle in response to Jesus' proclamation of the Kingdom of God.

To think and talk about:
- Peter left everything behind. Is such commitment only for a few? Even if he did literally leave everything behind in a physical sense, what things, e.g. his qualities and skills, could he not avoid taking with him as he followed Jesus?
- Talk about the things that you have 'left behind' and those things which remain with you as you follow Jesus.

John 1.35-42 (PURPLE and WHITE groups only)

John offers a quite different insight into the background of Peter's discipleship. He suggests that Peter's readiness to travel around Palestine in search of spiritual truth does not begin with his encounter with Jesus. Before Jesus comes on the scene we find Peter with his brother Andrew and an unnamed friend somewhere in the south of the country on the eastern bank of the River Jordan. They are part of the movement associated with John the Baptist. (The exact location of the 'Bethany' mentioned in John 1.28 is now unknown.)

If John reflects important historical information, it needs to be understood that his story is almost certainly constructed in such a way as to introduce theological themes to those who are reading the gospel. For example, John appears to make a concerted effort to present Peter in a different light. Peter still holds a prominent position in John's telling of the gospel story, but that position always seems to be counter-balanced by other disciples.

Verses 35-37

The scene begins with John the Baptist and two of his disciples, one of whom is later named as Andrew, Peter's brother (verse 40). Like many rabbis and religious leaders of the time, John attracted a group of disciples or learners, who would spend time with him listening to and following his teaching. John directs them to Jesus, describing him as the 'Lamb of God'. This phrase evokes echoes of a number of Old Testament passages, such as the lamb sacrificed at the Passover (Exodus 12), and the lamb 'about to be slaughtered' of Isaiah 53.7. The disciples respond by leaving John and following Jesus.

Verses 38-39

The conversation between Jesus, Andrew and his friend can be read at a quite superficial, everyday level. Jesus finds two people following him, and he asks them, 'What are you looking for?' Their first wish, quite naturally, is to get to know Jesus a bit better, and so they ask, 'Where do you live?' or, 'Where are you staying?' Jesus replies, 'Come and see.'

One always has the suspicion with John's gospel that nothing is to be taken at face value. Contemplating each of these questions takes us into the heart of Christian living. What are we looking for? Where do we find Jesus living in the world? Following Jesus is always more than 'come and listen' or 'come and learn'; it is 'come and see' – the Word is made flesh.

Verses 40-42

The other three gospels introduce Peter as the first of the disciples called by Jesus. In John's gospel it is Andrew who is given this privilege. What is more, he is also the first to confess Jesus as the Messiah, as he enthusiastically encourages his brother to come with him to meet Jesus. The order of events seems to stand in stark contrast to the other gospels where Peter always seems to be the 'first'.

The only thing which John records of the meeting between Jesus and Peter is Jesus' greeting. Without being introduced, Jesus immediately identifies Peter. In the act of naming him, it is as if Jesus says, 'I know your past (you are Simon son of John); and I know your future (you will be called Cephas).' Cephas and Peter both mean 'rock', as we have seen in the introduction and as John makes clear. Although Peter is not the first disciple to be mentioned in this gospel, his future prominence and role are still recognized by John. The nickname is here given as a promise for the future: this character who seems somewhat unstable will become rock-like.

To think and talk about:
- Note the differences between Luke's account of the call of Peter and John's account.
- Which elements of the stories are most like our present-day experiences of meeting and following Jesus?

FOUNDATION STONE
TO STUMBLING BLOCK (DECLARATION)

Matthew 16.13-18 (All groups)

The part which language, or self-expression, plays in the development of a person and in the building of relationships, should never be under-estimated. All conversation is important. Even a seemingly trivial exchange of words can help to cement relationships.

Occasionally a single sentence, or even a single word, effects a quantum leap in personal development or in the growth of a relationship. The ecstatic delight of parents when their child says, 'Mummy' or 'Daddy' for the first time is not sentimental self-indulgence. Something truly significant for the child and for the parents has taken place. When two people have fallen in love, the first nervous utterance of the words, 'I love you', not only describes the relationship, it actually affects it. Both the person who has spoken the words and the one who is addressed are altered. A bridge has been crossed.

To think and talk about:
Talk about your own experiences of the effects of putting things into words.

This passage concerns one such significant moment in Peter's growth in faith. He now puts into words the thoughts which have been going round in his mind as he has observed and followed Jesus. Prompted by Jesus' question, he addresses Jesus directly: 'You are the Messiah, the Son of the living God.' So much now changes for Peter. Jesus immediately affirms the part which Peter is to play among his future people (verse 18). But his confession also opens the door to a whole new set of uncertainties. Peter must have thought he had the answers neatly sewn up. However, he finds himself with all kinds of fresh questions to sort through.

Verse 13

This incident takes place near Caesarea Philippi, a city on the lower slopes of Mount Hermon, some 40 kilometres north of the sea of Galilee. The city had been built by Herod Philip, who named it after both the emperor and (modestly) himself.

The area was largely populated by non-Jews. This could have given Jesus the opportunity to spend time with the disciples on his own. He asks them what people are saying about him. In this context, the title 'Son of Man' is simply Jesus' way of referring to himself (cf. Matthew 8.20).

Verse 14

The answers which the disciples give show that all sorts of rumours and discussions are going around about Jesus' identity. Jesus has made people sit up and think. If the replies reflect popular responses to Jesus, they also reflect the extraordinarily speculative flavour of religious ideas at the time. People entertained all sorts of different notions as to how God was going to act to sort out the mess in which his people found themselves.

● Herod, of all people, is reported to have thought that Jesus was John the Baptist 'come back to life' (Matthew 14.2).

● There was a widely-held view that the prophet Elijah would return before the Messiah, and would be the one to anoint the Messiah for his mission. For people to be saying that Jesus was Elijah was therefore only one step short of claiming that he was the Messiah.

● To think of Jesus as 'Jeremiah or some other prophet' was also high acclaim. It was thought that there would be no more prophets until the dawning of the age of the Messiah.

Jesus had such an impact on people, both through his miracles and by his authoritative teaching, that they had begun to wonder whether the coming of the Messiah might be near.

Verses 15-16

Jesus now addresses the question directly to the disciples. He puts them on the spot. By doing so he helps them to take a further step in their developing journey of faith. He creates the opportunity for them to put into words the convictions which are beginning to form in their minds.

> **To think and talk about:**
> **Better out than in!**
> Moments of public profession are important in the development of faith:
> - by making public what has previously been held in private;
> - by drawing out convictions which we hadn't realized were there;
> - by helping us to stop wavering and make up our minds;
> - by enabling moments of self-recognition – it is sometimes only when we have to say where we stand that we actually 'know' where we stand;
> - by making us move from talking *about* faith to confessing faith.
>
> Talk about your experiences of 'going public' on your faith. Why and when can it be difficult? Why is it important for us?

Jesus is also laying a foundation for taking the disciples one stage further in their understanding of who he is and what it means to follow him. He draws out from them a kind of 'position statement' about where they are, knowing that he now wants to take them further.

The question which is addressed to all of the disciples is answered by Peter. There can be no doubt that Peter speaks for himself although it is possible that he is also answering on behalf of the other disciples. There are times when he seems to be the mouthpiece for all of them. Peter could have made no greater claim for Jesus. The Jewish people anticipated the time when God's promised Messiah (literally, 'anointed one') would come to re-establish God's reign in Israel. With the deep sense of outrage at the Roman occupation, this hope had taken on a distinctly political flavour. The phrase 'Son of the living God' (which is not found in the versions of the story told by Mark and Luke) may also have its background in the Jewish hope of a Messiah. There is evidence that the title 'Son of God' was used to describe the Messiah in Judaism at that time. It is, of course, difficult to read these words without thinking of all that the phrase 'Son of God' came to mean later in the Church, referring to Jesus' divine origin and nature.

In each of the first three gospels, this incident is related as being the first occasion when any of the disciples dares to make this claim for Jesus in such a direct way. As we have seen, John allows the story to be told in a rather different way. However, he still retains an episode where Peter confesses faith in Jesus at a time when many others are deserting him: 'Now we believe and know that you are the Holy One who has come from God' (John 6.69). Peter stands out in the memory of the Early Church for his early realization of Jesus' identity, and his readiness to give voice to his belief.

Verses 17-18

Matthew includes a number of stories about Peter which are not to be found in the other gospels. These next verses are found only in Matthew's version of this story. They have been the focus of much debate in the Church through the centuries, and form one of the scriptural sources of the great divide between the Roman Catholic and Protestant Churches. The Roman Catholic understanding of the authority of the Pope, as the successor of Peter, is based on the words of Jesus found here. We will not be able to look at these verses without being aware of this context.

Verse 17

'Good for you,' is the same phrase which is used at the beginning of the Beatitudes, and means, 'How happy are...' or 'Blessed are...' It is probably meant to convey a great deal more than 'Well done'. It describes the situation of those who find themselves in a right relationship with God, which is exactly what Jesus goes on to say about Peter. Jesus tells Peter that his deep insight has come to him as a gift from God. In whatever way Peter has come to this conclusion – whether as a result of logical deduction, a leap of intuition, or listening to what others were saying – Jesus assures him that the prompting of God is behind it all.

Verse 18

Matthew tells us that it is in response to his confession that Peter is given this new name (or title) by Jesus. We need to go back to the Aramaic to catch the full force of the play on words which Jesus uses: 'You are *Kepha*, and on this *kepha* I will build my church.' The word-play doesn't come off as well in Greek, because the two words for rock are slightly different: 'You are *Petros* and on this *petra* I will build my church.'

We can identify four main ways in which this much-discussed verse has been interpreted in the course of Christian history:

● From a fairly early period, it was understood as Peter's appointment by Jesus to a position of pre-eminent authority in the Early Church. As the Church debated structures of authority in the early centuries, the view began to emerge that Peter's pre-eminent position could and should be taken over by others, and in particular by those who succeeded to the position of bishop of Rome. This verse- and those which follow were seen to give biblical sanction to the supreme position of the Pope.

● The interpretation of this verse became critical for the leaders of the Reformation. They changed the focus from Peter to his act of confession. The use of two different words for rock in the Greek (*petros* and *petra*) allowed the

Reformers to claim that Jesus was not speaking about building his Church on Peter at all. The second word, petra, they claimed, does not refer to Peter himself, but to Peter's confession. Their conclusion was that the Church is built upon the confession of Peter and on the subsequent confessions of faith by all of those believers who followed in his footsteps.

- Towards the end of the nineteenth century it became popular among scholars to suggest that this verse is not an authentic saying of Jesus at all, but finds its origins in the Early Church. The main reason for this is that Jesus hardly ever has anything to say about the community of followers which he founded, and certainly not about any institutional structures in that community. The word 'church' (Greek 'ekklesia') is found on Jesus' lips only twice, both instances being in Matthew (here and Matthew 18.17). These sayings, it is argued, are more likely to have arisen out of the life of the Early Church, because Jesus was more interested in proclaiming the Kingdom of God than in forming the 'church of Jesus'.

- A fourth interpretation of this verse is that Jesus is speaking of Peter himself as the rock on which his Church would be built, but without any consequences for the institutional structure of the Church. Those who understand the words of Jesus in this way point to the remarkably similar words found in rabbinical writings, where Abraham is referred to as the rock on which God would build and found the world. As Abraham is a 'one off', so is Peter in the life of the Church.

What is important in this way of hearing Jesus' words is the meaning that we give to the word 'church' on Jesus' lips. It is difficult for us to hear 'church' without thinking of all of the institutional baggage which goes with it: ministers, bishops, church meetings, synods, moderators and so on and so forth. However, Jesus could easily have used this word to mean 'people of God', or 'community of God's people', without any preconceived ideas about structures – more of a movement than an institution.

This interpretation gives room for considerable irony – that it is Peter, of all people, who will be the bedrock on which the community of God's people will be formed. This says something about the change which Jesus brings to Peter's life. This unpredictable character becomes the dependable foundation of the community. It also says something about the nature of the community which Jesus inspires, perhaps best summed up by Paul: 'From the human point of view few of you were wise or powerful or of high social standing. God purposely chose what the world considers nonsense in order to shame the wise, and he chose what the world considers weak in order to shame the powerful' (1 Corinthians 1.26-27).

Jesus emphasizes the resilience of this community founded on Peter, by adding that 'not even death will ever be able to overcome it.' The community which forms around Jesus is to be a community in which the power of life always predominates, even over the ultimate forces of death. The phrase translated as 'death' here is literally 'the gates of Hades', that is, the gateway to the realm of the dead.

Verses 19-24 (GREEN, BLUE, PURPLE and WHITE groups)

Verse 19

Attention now turns from the gates of Hades to the doors of the Kingdom. Jesus entrusts Peter with the keys to the Kingdom of heaven. To be given the keys is a sign of great trust. If the gates of Hades symbolize death, so the doors of the Kingdom of heaven stand for life. Peter's mission will be to open the door to life. This is in stark contrast to Jesus' estimation of the Pharisees who 'lock the door to the Kingdom of heaven in people's faces' (Matthew 23.13).

What is more, Peter is given the task of 'prohibiting' and 'permitting' (literally 'binding' and 'loosing'). This can be understood in two ways. Either it means interpreting the law of God, giving authoritative guidance on what is right and wrong (much as the scribes would have done); or it means the power to forgive or to withhold forgiveness. The second of these perhaps fits better with the idea of Peter holding the keys of the Kingdom, but the first is also possible.

Elsewhere we find that the authority to bind and loose and to forgive or withhold forgiveness is given to the other disciples as well (Matthew 18.18 and John 20.23). Peter may receive these responsibilities first, but they are responsibilities which he shares with the body of the disciples.

If Peter has expressed his embryonic faith in Jesus, there is also a sense in which we can talk about Jesus showing faith in Peter. He entrusts to Peter, as he will to his other followers, awesome responsibilities in offering the Gospel of life and forgiveness to the world. How this all-too-fallible Peter acts in the future will have life-and-death consequences for people.

Verse 20

Jesus now tells his disciples not to announce to the world what they have come to believe about his Messiahship. The reason for this secrecy comes out in the next verses. Peter has certainly used the right word, but he is a long way from understanding all of the implications of what he has said. If the disciples have got the wrong end of the stick, how much more will the wider public.

Verses 21-22

Now that Jesus' identity as the Messiah is out in the open with his disciples, he takes them through the painful and difficult process of helping them to unlearn much of what they have been taught to associate with the Messiah. He prepares them for the inevitable destiny which is before him: not popular acclaim, political power, military victory or successful religious leadership; but suffering and death, and the strange, if not eccentric, hope of being raised to life.

Peter's new-found self-esteem perhaps goes to his head. He dares to take Jesus on one side in an attempt to put him right. Suffering and death at the hands of the Jerusalem élite just do not fit with Peter's preconceived ideas of what it means to be the Messiah. When he confessed Jesus as the Messiah he had quite different ideas in his mind. The strength of Peter's feelings is reflected in his words. He doesn't simply ask Jesus to think again.

Verse 23

Suddenly Peter is hero turned villain. Echoes of the earlier words of Jesus are to be found.

● No longer is he 'blessed by God,' but he is 'Satan'. He comes across to Jesus as the very voice of the tempter drawing him away from his true mission.

● The 'Rock', who before was to be the foundation of the Church, is now a stumbling block ('obstacle') in the path of Jesus.

● The one who earlier had spoken words inspired by God, is now speaking all-too-human words.

To think and talk about:
Same words, different meanings
Explore the words we use today to say what we believe about Jesus, and the way those words can mean different things to different people. How do we discern the most appropriate meaning?
e.g. Jesus is Lord   Jesus is Saviour   Jesus loves

Verse 24

Jesus now says to his disciples that if the path which he must follow involves suffering and sacrifice, so too will the path of those who follow him.

'forget self'   Jesus invites his followers to a lifestyle which is self-forgetful. The selflessness of the Christian way of life has a double emphasis. It is turning from a self-obsessed life to a life devoted to God; it is turning from a self-interested life to a life lived for the sake of others.

'carry his cross'   This phrase would have shocked Jesus' disciples. Criminals and rebels were crucified, and were forced to carry their crosses to the place of execution. It speaks of humiliation and defeat. It conveys an image of excruciating pain. Jesus is saying more than, 'Are you prepared for this to be your fate in the future?' He is saying that 'cross-carrying' is a mark of everyone who chooses to follow him. It fills out what Jesus means by 'forgetting self'. At its very least it means that those who follow Jesus will be prepared to identify with and come alongside people who live with humiliation, defeat and pain.

'and follow me'   The invitation which Peter and the disciples heard at the beginning of Jesus' Galilean ministry is now repeated. The confession, 'You are the Christ, the Son of the living God,' is not the end of the search. Indeed it is all the more important that the disciples learn to follow Jesus, now that they have begun to realize who he is. Discipleship is far more than a matter of 'right words' and 'right belief'. Jesus leads us in the way of self-forgetful, cross-carrying love.

Matthew 14.22-33 (PURPLE and WHITE groups)

One of the stories which Matthew includes about Peter, and which is not found in the other gospels, is the story of Peter walking on the water. (Mark and John include the story of Jesus walking on the water, but not the additional element of Peter's failed attempt.) There are several remarkable parallels between this story and the events at Caesarea Philippi. Both are stories of Jesus alone with his disciples. Both have Peter standing out from the rest of the disciples. Both show Peter stepping out in faith, only to find his feet taken from under him. Both are 'confession stories': but at Caesarea Philippi it happens in the course of a conversation, whereas here it takes place in almost surreal drama in the middle of the Galilean lake.

This story may relate an actual historical incident which took place in just this way. Alternatively it may have emerged in the story-telling tradition of the Early Church to express the relationship of a vulnerable church community to its risen Lord in a hostile world. We do not know; this question needs to be left to the conscience of the reader. Whichever position we take, the story is a powerful expression of the faith-experience of the early Christians.

Verses 22-24

The scene is set for the mid-lake encounter. Jesus, anxious for solitude in prayer, sends the disciples across the lake in the boat and dismisses the crowd. Matthew paints a sweeping, panoramic view of the solitary figure of Jesus at prayer in vast hills, and the tiny, vulnerable fishing craft in the middle of the lake, battling against the waves stirred up by the buffeting winds.

Verses 25-26

As with most dramatic stories in the New Testament, the events are narrated with an incredible economy of style. No explanations are attempted. Few details emerge. It is enough to be told that Jesus comes walking on the water in the long, weary hours before dawn, and of the resulting terror of the disciples. Their immediate reaction is that they are seeing a ghost.

Verse 27

Jesus' words of reassurance to the terror-filled boat-load of disciples come with the ring of divine authority:

- they echo the words of God to Joshua, 'Don't be afraid or discouraged...' (Joshua 1.9); and to the people of Israel through the prophet Isaiah of Babylon, 'Do not be afraid – I will save you' (Isaiah 43.1);

- the phrase 'it is I' is the translation of the Greek 'ego eimi', which can also be the translation of the mysterious name of God, 'I AM' (Exodus 3.14);

- the words 'Do not be afraid' are found on Jesus' lips in Matthew's gospel when the divine presence shines through his life – here as he walks on water, on the mountain of transfiguration (Matthew 17.7) and outside the empty tomb (Matthew 28.10).

Verses 28-30

Peter's impulsive reaction to the situation is indicative of his character. He voices a faith, enthusiastic in its trust in the power of Jesus. However, the initial flash of faithful dependence quickly wanes once Peter becomes aware of where he is, and the force of the wind blowing against him. It is interesting to note that Peter begins to sink, not because he suddenly becomes aware of the impossibility of walking on the water, but because he is afraid of the wind! His words of faith quickly evaporate once he is out of the boat and on the water. His faith gives way to fear, and he begins to sink. In his panic he cries out to Jesus to rescue him.

Verse 31

Jesus at once saves him, and rebukes him for his lack of faith. Yet again we find the New Testament writers unafraid to record the weakness and failings of Peter. He finds himself very much on the sharp end of Jesus' tongue, even though he gave faith a chance.

By including Peter's failed attempt to walk on the water, Matthew's version of this story emphasizes the seeming impossibility and vulnerability of Jesus' way in our world. These are the high demands of faith. Jesus, who walks on water, invites his disciples to follow him; Jesus, who takes up his cross, invites his disciples to follow.

Verses 32-33

The episode ends with the storm abating, and an astounded group of disciples, reunited with Jesus, awed into worship, and professing faith in Jesus as the 'Son of God'.

To think and talk about:
- Why do you think that we decided not to use this story with younger children?

A SHEEP RUNNING SCARED... (DENIAL)

Mark 14.1-2, 27-42, 66-72

Peter of the rash promise and the low endurance comes into his own when Jesus faces his last fateful days. For all that Jesus has prepared Peter for this moment, he seems ill-equipped as the events unfold. Peter, who at Caesarea Philippi had protested at Jesus' prediction of suffering and death, now reveals his continuing determination to push all thoughts of suffering to the back of his mind. Peter, who on the sea of Galilee had been overcome by fears, now, when put on the spot, finds fear once again dispelling faith. Yet before it all happens he vigorously protests his faithfulness to the point of death.

Verses 1-2 (All groups)

These verses introduce Mark's passion narrative. The events take place in the lead-up to the Festival of the Passover and Unleavened Bread, the Israelite's major festival celebrating their deliverance from slavery in Egypt. The lambs for the Passover meal were slaughtered on the afternoon of Nisan 14th. The Passover meal was eaten that evening, between sunset and midnight on Nisan 15th (the Jewish day starting at sunset). The feast of Unleavened Bread lasted for seven days, from Nisan 15th to Nisan 21st.

The death of Jesus is plotted by the two leading groups of the Jewish community. The chief priests were responsible for the worship, prayer and sacrificial rites of the temple. The teachers of the Law interpreted the Hebrew scriptures for the people, with a special emphasis on upholding and applying the laws of God as they had been interpreted from one generation to another. Those entrusted with sacrifice and those entrusted with scripture on behalf of God's people now join forces to execute God's Messiah.

The circumstances of the Festival make the arrest of Jesus a dangerous exercise. The combination of Jesus' popular acclaim and the festival of Israel's deliverance could become a volatile mixture if he is arrested in public. The reluctance to arrest Jesus 'during the festival' could be taken to mean a reluctance to arrest him 'in front of the festival crowd.' In the light of what transpires, this makes more sense.

Verses 27-31 (All groups)

The day of the Passover festival arrives. Judas has agreed to betray Jesus (verses 10-11), and Jesus has eaten the Passover Meal with the twelve (verses 12-25). Having sung a hymn, they leave for the Mount of Olives.

In these verses, both Peter and the reader are prepared for the looming drama of denial. It was potentially an embarrassment, if not a scandal for the Early Church. These verses place Peter's personal story of failure in the context of a wider story which is being played out.

Verses 27-28

● The desertion of the disciples is no surprise to Jesus. He knows beforehand that the heat of the situation will drive them away.

● Peter's failure is one story alongside the stories of the other disciples who were also to desert Jesus at this critical time.

● The death of the shepherd and the scattering of the sheep are prefigured in the pages of the Hebrew scriptures. The quotation is from Zechariah 13.7. It was clearly comforting to the Early Church that their scriptures hinted at the strange ways of God at work in the events of the arrest and crucifixion of Jesus. Although there is an inevitability in the events, this does not lessen the responsibility of the individuals involved.

● The scattering of the sheep and the slaughter of the shepherd do not represent the end of the story. Jesus predicts his resurrection, and hints at the gathering together of the flock in Galilee. All of this must have seemed like a riddle to the disciples.

Verses 29-31

Peter believes that he is different from all of the others. He is convinced that he can stay the course. Jesus responds by saying that Peter will indeed be singled out in the coming hours:

● not by hanging in there longer than any others; what will happen is imminent, in the next few hours, indeed before the cock crows;

● not only will he desert Jesus, he will actually deny any knowledge of him;

- he will do so not once, but three times.

Peter becomes more vigorous in his protestations of loyalty. Angered by the suggestion that he could ever deny knowing Jesus, he declares that he would die before doing so. The rest of the disciples pledge the same loyalty.

To think and talk about:
- Do you think Peter's protestations were all 'front'?
- Did he believe what he was saying?
- Talk about situations in which you have had to 'eat your words'.

Verses 32-42 (GREEN, BLUE, PURPLE and WHITE groups)

Verse 32

Gethsemane is situated somewhere on the Mount of Olives. Its name means 'olive press', which suggests that it was probably an olive grove. It has come to be known as the 'Garden of Gethsemane' because John describes the place of Jesus' arrest as a 'garden' (John 18.1), although he does not name the spot as Gethsemane.

Jesus comes here to pray. From Luke and John, we find that this was a regular place of seclusion for Jesus and his disciples (see Luke 22.39 and John 18.2).

Verses 33-34

At significant moments during his ministry, Jesus separates Peter, James and John from the other disciples. He does so now, seemingly for their close presence during a time of immense 'distress and anguish'. These words express the sense of horror and anxiety which gripped Jesus as he faced what was before him.

Together with James and John, Peter finds Jesus confiding in him, laying bare the deep anguish which he feels. Jesus treats Peter as one would a close friend, unburdening himself in the face of the impending horror of his death. He asks Peter, James and John to stay near him, and remain watchful.

Many scholars have noted the contrast between the manner in which Jesus faced his death and the joyful courage reported of many Christian martyrs. Martin Luther makes the comment: 'No one ever feared death so much as this Man.' Far from 'rising above' the fear of death in some heroic or stoical way, Jesus feels the fear, the sorrow, and the estrangement of death acutely.

Verses 35-36

Jesus goes only a short distance away from the three. Lying face down on the ground for prayer indicates an intensity in Jesus' impassioned searching of God's will.

Jesus is willing to suffer, not because he believes there is some nobility to be found in bearing pain, but simply because it is God's will. He does not want to suffer the agony of the cross. His overwhelming desire is to be obedient to the One he addressed with intimacy as 'Abba' (Father). If such obedience calls for crucifixion, then that is the path he will take. When Jesus uses the phrase 'cup of suffering', he reveals the full dimensions of the horror which is before him. This phrase is a shorthand version of 'the cup of God's anger' which is found in the Hebrew scriptures. For example, Psalm 75.8: 'The Lord holds a cup in his hand, filled with the strong wine of his anger.' Jesus cannot see his death purely in terms of human tragedy and a breakdown in human relationships. God is deeply involved in the events and relationships as well; Jesus perceives that, by suffering, in some mysterious way he is sharing in God's holy and righteous anger against sin.

Verses 37-38

The hoped-for support of the disciples is not forthcoming. Jesus returns to find them asleep. All three are sleeping, but Jesus' remarks are addressed specifically to Peter. For all that Jesus spoke beforehand of the desertion of the disciples, his disappointment now at their lethargy is evident. He urges them to prayer. Indeed he encourages them to enter into his own prayer to be saved from temptation and to follow the way of obedience.

'The spirit is willing, but the flesh is weak,' contains disappointment, affirmation and understanding in more or less equal measure. He is disappointed that at such a critical moment the disciples allow themselves to be overcome by tiredness; he affirms their inner desire to remain true to him. He also understands what it is like to be pulled in two directions.

Verses 39-42

Jesus returns a second time, and again finds them asleep. One senses the disciples' inner shame at being found so inadequate.

He offers a third opportunity for them to be near and support him in these agonizing moments, if only by doing him the courtesy of keeping awake. When Jesus returns the third and final time, he finds them still sleeping and resting. As he wakes them this time, he rouses them to meet those who are coming to arrest him.

Having faced his fear, Jesus knows that all that is happening is within God's purposes. 'The hour has come' – the hour for fulfilling God's will. When Jesus says, 'Let us go', the words can have a military feel to them: 'Let us advance to meet them.' In the intensity of his prayer, and through the unfolding of events, Jesus knows where obedience will now lead him.

Verses 66-72 (All groups)

Jesus, betrayed by Judas, is arrested and taken to the High Priest's house for an impromptu midnight trial. Verse 54 tells us that Peter finds his way to the courtyard of the house, and sits down with the guards by the fire.

Verses 66-67
The High Priest's house is probably of Roman style, built around four sides of a courtyard. Verse 66 suggests that the trial of Jesus takes place in a first-floor room overlooking the courtyard. Peter is spotted by one of the servant girls, who recognizes him as one of Jesus' followers. The writer emphasizes the fact that 'she looked straight at him'. Held by her stare, Peter is confronted with the truthful observation, 'You, too, were with him.'

Had he been asked a direct question, Peter might have felt easier. He is unnerved and confused by such a bald statement of fact. He pleads ignorance and goes out to the passage, possibly the entrance area opening onto the court at the front of the house.

The report of the cock crowing at this point is not found in all of the manuscripts of the gospel. The question which has to be asked is whether it is more likely that someone copying the manuscript would leave it out or add it in. Many people think it more likely that it has been added to ensure that both instances of the cock crowing are recorded.

Verses 69-70
Unfortunately the servant girl sees Peter in his new location. This time she speaks not to Peter but to the bystanders. Once again he finds himself denying his association with Jesus.

The third time it is the bystanders who start to accuse Peter. His Galilean origin gives the game away. Matthew records that it is Peter's northern accent which reveals his origins (Matthew 26.73). There is no reason why a Galilean should not be in Jerusalem, especially at Passover time but, given the heightened tension of the situation and the lateness of the hour, it is understandable that people jump to the conclusion that he has come to Jerusalem with Jesus.

Verse 71

Peter's responses have been gradually increasing in intensity. Now he loses his cool. He swears; he calls down curses from God; he disclaims all knowledge of Jesus.

Verse 72

Peter is caught in a spiralling situation, which began with him simply avoiding the unwanted attention of the servant, and escalated to this outright dissociation. It is easy to imagine his shame the moment he hears the cock crowing. It has all got out of control. He is left in tears.

To think and talk about:
- Do you have sympathy with Peter? How do your own experiences help you to relate to what Peter was going through?
- What do you think made him linger in the courtyard?
- Why do you think he disowned Jesus?
- Would Jesus' warnings have made the situation more bearable or more painful for Peter?
- Would you have gone with Peter into the courtyard?

... TO SHEPHERD OF THE FLOCK (RESTORATION)

John 21.1-19

This resurrection appearance of Jesus is recorded only by John. It bears a remarkable resemblance to the story of the miraculous catch of fish which Luke describes as part of the episode in which Peter was called to discipleship. Some believe that both stories can be traced back to the same incident, with the narrative developing in different ways as it was passed on and used in preaching and teaching in different church contexts. Others consider that there were two quite separate incidents. Whichever view one adopts, the two stories now differ considerably in content and intention.

To do together:
Spot the difference!
Make a pictorial chart to show the differences between the story in Luke 5.1-11 and the story in John 21.1-17.

John 21.1-17 (All groups)

Verse 1
The location is given as 'Lake Tiberias', another name for Lake Galilee. The story is introduced as a resurrection appearance.

Verses 2-3
Seven disciples are mentioned. As usual Peter heads the list of names. Only John names Nathanael as one of the twelve. This is the only time in the gospel of John that the 'sons of Zebedee' (James and John) are specifically referred to.

John does not explain why the disciples have come back to Galilee. In Mark and Matthew, the disciples are told to go there to await the appearance of the risen Lord. It reads here as if they have simply gravitated homewards, not sure what to do with themselves in these early post-crucifixion, post-resurrection days. That feeling is only amplified by Peter's decision to go fishing. He is probably the kind of person who has to be doing something.

The others join him for want of anything else to do. The unproductive day, however, is followed by an unproductive night. As in Luke's story, they catch nothing.

Verses 4-6

A common thread running through many of the post-resurrection appearance stories is that Jesus is not recognized by his followers. Mary Magdalene thought he was the gardener. The couple on the road to Emmaus talked with him as with a stranger. This theme could well have been treasured in the telling of the stories, because it rang bells with the way in which the early Christians were constantly surprised by the hidden presence of the risen Lord in people and in places where he was least expected.

According to Luke, Peter agreed to throw the nets out one more time only because it was Jesus who asked him. On this occasion the disciples take the word of the stranger on the seashore, not knowing that it is Jesus. It is said that occasionally shoals of fish in Lake Galilee can be seen from the shore more easily than from a boat.

The size of the catch is such that the fishermen are unable to haul it in. Again this contrasts with the story in Luke, where the nets began to break and the fish were piled into the boats.

Verse 7

John sets alongside Peter another (unnamed) disciple 'whom Jesus loved.' Their responses typify their respective characters. The beloved disciple is the quicker of the two to perceive and to believe. As soon as he sees the size of the catch, the penny drops and he recognizes Jesus. Peter, however, is the first to act. He hears the other disciple's exclamation, picks up his outer garment and plunges into the water to get ashore. John seems to want to balance two different influences on the Church: that of Peter's activist character and the more insightful and reflective influence of the beloved disciple.

It seems rather odd to us that Peter should get dressed to jump into the water! The explanation is probably to be found in the realm of etiquette. Peter jumps into the water in order to make his way to the shore and greet Jesus. The act of greeting was thought of as a religious one and so could not be performed naked.

Verses 8-10

When the disciples wade ashore, Jesus already has a charcoal fire burning. Indeed there is fish cooking before they arrive. It is possible that two stories have been combined here, one speaking of Jesus providing the fish, the other of the disciples providing them.

Verse 11

It is Peter, the 'doer', who is portrayed here as being the only one to respond to Jesus' request for fish. What is more, he single-handedly drags ashore the net bulging with fish. This scene captures the way in which Peter was remembered in the early Christian community, not so much as a fisherman, but as the leader of the Church's evangelistic enterprise, 'catching people'.

It is thought that the number of fish caught (153) has symbolic meaning. One suggestion takes note of the fact that 153 is the sum of all the numbers from 1 to 17. The number 17, being itself the sum of the 'complete' numbers 10 and 17, is symbolic of absolute completeness. Another theory draws on the observation that ancient naturalists identified 153 different varieties of fish. Both of these theories point to a similar conclusion: that the Gospel message is for all.

Verse 12

Apparently there are all sorts of questions going around in the disciples' minds as Jesus invites them to eat breakfast with him. Even the searching question, 'Who are you?', is not far from the surface. Yet intuitively they know that they are in the presence of the Lord. Awe and wonder alone may prevent them from questioning him.

Verse 13

The sharing of bread and fish is told with the same simple dignity as the descriptions of the Last Supper. The beach breakfast is charged with the memories of the feeding of the five thousand and the eucharistic celebration.

Verse 14

This editorial comment interrupts the flow of the story.

Verses 15-17

Jesus now confronts Peter alone. Three times Peter had fallen asleep in the garden. Three times Peter had denied all connection with Jesus. Now three times Jesus asks Peter to confess his love for him. There can be no doubt that Jesus is helping Peter to deal with his past – but he does so without dragging it up, or raking over the details.

This is no 'de-briefing' session. Jesus does not sit down with Peter and analyse what went wrong. Simply by asking the question three times, Jesus is tacitly saying, 'We both know what happened, don't we?' But the experiences of the garden and the High Priest's courtyard are left firmly in the past. The question is about the present: 'Do you love me?' The issue at stake is who Peter will be in the future: 'Take care of my sheep.' The one who had cowered and fled like a scared sheep is now being commissioned as a shepherd of the flock.

To think and talk about:
This is a story full of emotion. To try to get into the scene, play around with the dialogue between Jesus and Peter by using different tones of voice. Do different members of the group imagine the conversation in different ways?

Verse 15

The first time Jesus poses the question, he asks Peter to compare his love with that of his fellow disciples: 'Do you love me more than these others do?' The question, phrased in this way, could well be a pointed reference back to Peter's rather arrogant assertion that he was different from the rest of the disciples. They might desert Jesus, but he would never do so. It is possible that Jesus is not asking Peter to claim a greater love than his fellow-disciples. Rather he is saying, 'Well now, Peter, given all that has happened, can you really claim to love me more than these others do?'

In his response, Peter certainly makes no effort to enter into any competition with his friends. All he can assert is his own love for Jesus. He makes his appeal to Jesus' intuitive knowledge of those around him: 'You know that I love you.'

The charge to tend the lambs is a commission to leadership in the Christian community, a leadership based on the exercise of care and compassion. The image of a 'shepherd' for the leaders of the people in the Old Testament was used largely when they were accused by the prophets of their failure to care for the weak and the vulnerable (see especially Ezekiel 34). Peter, the activist fisher of men, is now being charged with the complementary role of the shepherd's care.

This story is often described as the 'restoration' or 'rehabilitation' of Peter. Such descriptions are somewhat misleading, because they imply that Peter is merely restored to the relationship he had with Jesus prior to his denial. Nothing can be further from the truth. The whole experience of denial and desertion of the crucified Jesus, encounter with the risen one, and confession of love, takes Peter into a depth of relationship with Jesus which he has not known before. Jesus does not ask him to repeat assertions and confessions made previously. His direct question, 'Do you love me?' draws Peter into a new chapter of faithful response. This question goes beyond, 'Who do you say I am?', but it can only be answered by Peter now, on the other side of the cock-crow and the cross.

Verse 16

The second time Jesus asks the question, no comparison is made with the other disciples. This seems to confirm that Jesus is looking for Peter's affirmation of love, not for a stronger love in Peter than in the other disciples.

Verse 17

Some commentators have suggested that it is significant that on the third occasion John has Jesus using a different (Greek) word for love (*philo* rather than *agapo*) – a supposedly weaker form of love. This, they contend, accounts for Peter's annoyance. He is offended that Jesus should need to ask him about this inferior friendship-love, let alone the committed love of *agape*. However, John has a habit of using different words to mean the same thing. Often through his gospel *philo* and *agapo* are used interchangeably. The change of word here is probably nothing more than a stylistic feature of John's writing.

As Peter had been overwhelmed with sorrow when the cock crowed and he realized what he had done, so now the third asking of the question fills him with sadness. The healing of the past is not without its pain. Perhaps Peter's protest at being asked the third time actually reveals that Peter knows that the question had to be asked the third time. Despite the sorrow and the protest, Jesus affirms Peter's place within the community of his followers in exactly the same way as before.

To think and talk about:
- Spend some time thinking about your own experiences of mending broken relationships: times when you have let others down badly; times when others have let you down.
- Talk about ways of coping with broken relationships.
- Can we learn any lessons from the way in which Jesus dealt with Peter?

Verses 18-19 (PURPLE and WHITE groups only)

There is a remarkable parallel between what follows and the sequence of events at Caesarea Philippi. There Peter confessed Jesus as the Christ, the Son of the living God. Jesus proceeded to affirm Peter's prominence in the Christian community and to speak of his own impending crucifixion, and then called the disciples to take up the cross and follow. Here Peter confesses his love of Jesus, who enrols him in the task of caring for his sheep, and then predicts Peter's own eventual death, bearing witness to his faith.

It is possible that a proverb underlies this verse: 'In youth, man goes free, where he wishes; in old age he must allow himself to be led, even where he does not wish.'

The second part of the proverb, however, has been substantially changed. The proverb speaks of the restrictions of age. Jesus' talk of the stretching out and binding of hands would have been understood by the early Christians as a reference to crucifixion. This is confirmed in the explanatory note which follows. The readers are intended to infer from these words the manner of Peter's death. Just as John interpreted the death of Jesus as the glorification of God, so he now says that Peter will 'bring glory to God' by his death.

There is a strong tradition that Peter was indeed martyred, suffering death by crucifixion in Rome. However, there is little documentary evidence coming from either the first or the early part of the second century to confirm this. The gospel of John was almost certainly written after Peter's death, which means that this verse is probably the clearest evidence available for the manner of Peter's death. One tradition tells how Peter requested that he should be crucified with his head downwards.

The episode concludes with Jesus inviting Peter (for the third time!) to follow him. Perhaps now he has finally learned what it means to follow... and is ready to carry it through to the point of death.

FROM GOSPEL FOR SOME
TO GOSPEL FOR ALL (DEVELOPMENT)

Acts 11.1-18; 15.6-11

We have already followed Peter through momentous changes in his life. We have seen him turn his back on his fishing business to follow a miracle-working, wandering teacher. We have witnessed his seemingly outrageous leap of faith in confessing this man as the Messiah, and the challenge of having to think about messiahship from a wholly new standpoint. We have followed him through the events of the cross and resurrection, through the traumatic test and the eventual burgeoning of faith and friendship. The change which Peter now takes on board is no less momentous.

According to Luke's account of events in the book of Acts, Peter assumes the mantle of leadership from the beginning of the early Christian mission. It is Peter who takes the lead in appointing an apostle to replace Judas Iscariot (Acts 1.15-26). On the Day of Pentecost, Peter preaches the sermon which leads to the conversion of three thousand people (Acts 2.14-42). It is Peter who speaks for the apostles when they are brought before the Council (the Sanhedrin), the leading body of the Jews in Jerusalem (Acts 5.27-32). Peter and John are sent by the apostles in Jerusalem to preach the Gospel in Samaria. Through this ministry, the Samaritans receive the Holy Spirit (Acts 8.4-17). Peter, it seems, takes on more and more travelling, spear-heading the missionary thrust of the Church (Acts 9.32). By the time we come to the meeting of apostles and elders in Jerusalem in Acts 15 (see below) James, the brother of Jesus, has taken on the role of leadership in Jerusalem.

We need to understand that throughout the earliest period of the Christian mission, Christianity was a growing movement within Judaism. The leaders were Jews, declaring to their fellow-Jews that Jesus of Nazareth, the crucified and risen one, was the Messiah. The first 'converts' did not see themselves changing from one religion to another. Rather, they took on a new conviction about their own religion.

It is in this context that we need to set Peter's encounter with Cornelius (told fully in Acts 10 and reported by Peter to his fellow leaders in Jerusalem in this passage, Acts 11.1-18). The incident marks a sea-change in Peter's understanding of the Gospel, and sparks controversy in the Church. As Luke records the episode, Peter finds himself undergoing a fundamental shift of outlook, as the world of Jewish Christianity encounters the challenge of the mission to the Gentiles. The issue at stake is whether non-Jews who become convinced of the good news of Jesus need to become Jews in order to become Christians.

To think and talk about:
Changing what comes naturally
How difficult is it to change things that we take for granted? Use these ideas to get you thinking:
- Ask everyone to fold their arms. Notice which arm is over which. Then ask everyone to fold their arms the other way. How does it feel?
- Ask those in the group who can remember the decimalization of our currency in 1971 to talk about their experiences. Ask them whether they still convert back into shillings.
- Talk about metric weights and measures. How many people cope with buying goods in metric units? Do you still think and estimate in imperial measurements?

Verses 1-4 (GREEN, BLUE, PURPLE and WHITE groups)

The conversion of Cornelius and his household has stirred up a controversy. It has become the talking-point in the Christian community not only in Jerusalem, but throughout Judea. Luke clearly sees the whole episode as a significant turning-point in the history of the Early Church. The controversial nature of the events is brought out in a few telling phrases.

- 'The Gentiles also had received the word of God.' One might think that this would be a reason for rejoicing. However, it calls for a completely new outlook for these early Jewish Christians, who initially saw their mission as being to their fellow-Jews, not only in Jerusalem but throughout the world.

- 'Those who were in favour of circumcising Gentiles.' The Christian community is not altogether opposed to the idea of Gentiles becoming Christians. However, they assume that commitment to Jesus as the Messiah also entails becoming a Jew. It is not conceivable for someone to be baptized as a Christian without being circumcised as a Jew. They find it impossible to separate the two.

- 'You were a guest in the home of uncircumcised Gentiles.' The first Christians, it seems, continue to observe all the customs of their Jewish heritage, including the various food laws. The charge of being a guest in a Gentile's home probably implies a contravention of these food laws. Peter's encounter with Cornelius means that he has flouted these laws, making himself 'unclean'.

To think and talk about:
Clean and unclean
It is all too easy for us to treat other cultures as something of a curiosity, especially when it comes to customs connected with food. However, all societies and groups have social customs about what is appropriate or inappropriate behaviour, not all of which are easy for others to understand.

- Identify customs in our own society. You may like to think about language (where the terms 'clean' and 'unclean' are appropriate); ways of eating; dress-codes; acceptable and unacceptable behaviour.
- Think about sub-groups, for example youth cultures, where there are unwritten codes of what makes someone 'in' or 'out'.
- What about 'church culture'?

Peter offers to explain what has brought him to such a fundamental shift in outlook and attitudes.

Verses 5-10 (All groups)

Verses 5-6
The story begins with Peter in Joppa, a port on the Mediterranean coast, about 56 kilometres from Jerusalem (just south of modern-day Tel Aviv). He is staying with the small community of Christians in the city, lodging in the house of Simon the leather-worker (see Acts 9.42-43). Peter tells how the whole episode began with a vision which came to him while he was in prayer. Throughout the report Peter plays down his part in the proceedings, and highlights the initiative which came from God. He is keen to emphasize that his re-orientation was instigated by divine intervention. It is not the outcome of a long process of thought, or an expedient response to a difficult situation.

Verses 7-8
The instruction to kill and eat the animals could only have puzzled Peter, because many, if not all, of the animals would have been considered 'unclean' by a Jew. Peter lived according to the Old Testament food laws, which were quite specific about which animals were 'clean' and which were 'unclean' (see Leviticus 11 and Deuteronomy 14.3-21). To eat meat which is regarded as 'unclean' is to make oneself ritually 'unclean'.

This way of life may seem quite strange to people who do not have first-hand experience of Jewish practices. The food laws are based on the strongly-held conviction that the world is so ordered by God that the eating of certain animals is consistent with living in the realm of his holiness, whereas to eat other animals is to step outside that realm of holiness. No reason is given, for example, for the prohibition on eating pork. Different possibilities have been suggested for the origin of the custom. It could reflect Israel's nomadic roots (swine are not suitable for the nomadic lifestyle). Alternatively, it could be that the pig was extensively used as a sacrificial animal in Canaanite religions. It is a matter of conjecture. What is clear, however, is that the question of how to live in tune with God's holiness is never simply a matter of moral issues. It pervades the whole of life: the pattern of work, the clothes that are worn and the food that is eaten.

Initially Peter may have thought that the vision was some kind of test. All of his instincts and convictions tell him that it would be quite wrong to eat the animals before him. He refuses the invitation. To accept would go against all that he has lived for up to this point.

Verses 9-10

Although the whole episode is repeated twice, on each occasion Peter responds in the same way. He is not budged from his convictions which are second nature to him. The repetition emphasizes both the consistency of God in challenging Peter's stance, and the solidity of Peter's resolve.

The vision itself does not change Peter's thinking immediately. He finds himself somewhat puzzled as to its meaning (see Acts 10.17, 19). Its significance only emerges in the events which follow.

Verses 11-17 (GREEN, BLUE, PURPLE and WHITE groups)

Verses 11-12

Without the time to reflect on the vision or work out its meaning, Peter finds himself being invited by three visitors from Caesarea to go back with them to meet Cornelius, a Gentile and a captain in the Roman army. He relates how the Holy Spirit prompted him to accept the invitation. It is implied that without the Spirit's intervention Peter would have thought twice about doing so. We should avoid trying to explain this reluctance by over-simplifying the Jewish customs regarding contact with Gentiles. Simply meeting with a Gentile, or even being in the house of a Gentile, would not contravene any of the purity laws – especially as this particular person is described as 'God-fearing' (Acts 10.2) and supportive of the Jewish religion and people. In Peter's conversation with Cornelius (Acts 10.28), Luke seems to over-simplify the situation, probably to emphasize the dramatic change which takes place. The potential difficulty for Peter is that he may be offered food which it would be improper for him to eat, either because it is the wrong sort of meat, or because it has been used as a sacrifice in one of the Greek or Roman cults.

Peter does not travel to Caesarea alone. He takes with him six members of the Christian community from Joppa. We do not know a great deal about this community. There were already believers there when Peter came. His presence had been requested because one of their number, Tabitha (or Dorcas), had died. Peter, it is reported, restored her to life again, a miracle which drew others to the faith (Acts 9.36-43). Two clues suggest that this community brings together people from different social strata. There is the hint that Dorcas is a trader with financial resources to help those in need (see Acts 9.36 and 39). The other member of the community whose name we know is Simon the leather-worker, in whose house Peter is staying (Acts 9.43). Tanners were often treated with some disdain by others, largely because the nature of their job caused them to smell unpleasant. Furthermore, their constant contact with animal corpses and with urine which was used to treat the leather, made them 'unclean' in the eyes of the Jews.

Caesarea was further north on the Mediterranean coast. A Roman garrison was stationed there. Cornelius was a centurion in 'The Italian Regiment', which was possibly a battalion of archers. A centurion was an officer who had risen through the ranks, and who had a 80-100 men under his command. In Acts 10.2-4 we discover that he is a deeply religious person, involving himself in the worship, prayers and support of the local Jewish community.

Verses 13-14

We now hear from Cornelius' point of view how the events were directed by the Spirit of God. An angel (literally a 'messenger') gave him a message to send to Joppa for Peter. In the first version of the story (Acts 10.4-6) Cornelius is simply told to send servants to ask Peter to come. No reason is given for this. Now in the reported version, Cornelius is told to send for Peter so that he can preach and bring the message of God's salvation to Cornelius and his family. In this context, 'family' should probably be read as 'household', including not only Cornelius' relatives, but his servants as well.

Verse 15

In reporting the story, Peter says little of his preaching – in fact he implies that he was hardly able to get into his message before those who were listening were filled with the Holy Spirit in a dramatic way. Once again all of the moves are made by God and not by Peter. The effects of the presence of the Spirit on Cornelius and his household are compared to the apostles' experience 'at the beginning' – that is, on the day of Pentecost. In Luke's writings, the dramatic experiences which are associated with the coming of the Holy Spirit are consistently described for the sake of their impact on the witnesses. The experiences are not described in terms of either the benefit to the recipients, or their on-going role in the ministry of the Church. They simply bear witness in visible and audible ways that God has acted in a significant way.

Verse 16

Peter sees these events as the fulfilment of the words Jesus spoke just before his ascension. The closest version of this saying to be found on the lips of Jesus is recorded in Acts 1.5. The risen Jesus prepares his disciples for the events which will follow his ascension: 'John baptized with water, but in a few days you will be baptized with the Holy Spirit.'

Verse 17

Peter argues that if these Gentiles are baptized with the Holy Spirit, the distinctive seal of those who believe in Jesus, how can their status as fellow-believers be denied? To refuse baptism to Cornelius and his household would be to oppose God. For Peter and those with him, it is a radically new step to receive Gentiles into the community of faith without requiring their full obedience to the commands of the old covenant. However, God has so ordered the sequence of events that Peter can come to only one conclusion. Peter's vision, Cornelius' angelic visitation, the Spirit's prompting of Peter, the coming of the Spirit on Cornelius, and the words of Jesus all combine to overturn Peter's deepest inclinations as a faithful Jew seeking to follow Jesus.

Verse 18 (All groups)

Peter so convinces the gathering that they give their approval to his actions and recognize this momentous new development as a sign of God's universal grace. They realize that the opportunity for repentance and life in Christ is open to Gentiles as well as Jews. The only possible response is praise and worship. The conversion of Cornelius is the catalyst for the conversion of the Early Church to a new way of understanding God and the nature of the relationship between God and people.

To think and talk about:
A Personal Story
A few years ago I engaged in theological study on the place of children in the life of the Church. In the course of the study I found myself having to take children's growing faith and relationship with God much more seriously than before. This has had profound implications for my understanding of the nature of the Church, which I am still trying to work through.

I come from the Baptist tradition, which tends to draw a fairly clear line of demarcation around the Church. The members of the Church are those who have made a profession of faith, normally through believers' baptism. We talk about the Church as a 'fellowship of believers'. But now I have to ask, where do the children come into this equation? If children are not 'potential believers', or 'on the way towards faith', or 'believers in preparation', but if they have a faith which is appropriate to them, do they not also belong fully to the community of faith? If so, how do we make that clear?

These are now my questions. My theological framework has been jolted. Children have been 'my Cornelius'.
- Do you have a 'Cornelius experience'?

Acts 15.6-11 (PURPLE and WHITE groups only)

The conversion of Cornelius, followed by the flowering of Paul's mission to the Gentiles, marks the beginning of a turbulent period of dispute within the Early Church. Some Jewish Christians are not at all convinced that the laws of Moses can be set aside quite so easily. The dispute comes to a head in a meeting of the apostles and elders in Jerusalem, attended by Paul and Barnabas. The main point of contention is whether or not Gentile converts should be circumcised.

It is in the course of this debate that Peter makes his final appearance in the book of Acts. His speech reads as something of an endorsement of the key themes of Paul's mission, which now takes prominence in the spread of the Gospel. One has only to read Galatians 2.11-14 to see that relations between Paul and Peter were not always sweetness and light, and that Peter continued to struggle with relationships with Gentiles.

The eventual outcome of the debate is something of a compromise. The Gentiles are excused the demands of circumcision, but some of the food laws are to be maintained. They are not to eat food which has been sacrificed to idols, nor eat any animals which have been strangled, nor the blood of animals (Acts 15.19-21). Nonetheless, a sea-change has occurred which is irreversible. The ritual laws of the Old Testament are no longer binding on those who come to faith in Christ from a background of Gentile culture.

Verses 6-7

Peter has certainly changed through the years, if this account is at all accurate. He is no longer the rash Peter who is the first to speak out. He has now become the elder statesman figure who allows argument and counter-argument to be put before he makes his decisive contribution. He is still portrayed as the spokesperson for the apostles.

He reminds his listeners that it was God who called him to bring the Gospel to the Gentiles. He can only be referring here to the conversion of Cornelius. This was his moment of calling to a new mission.

Verses 8-9

For Peter, the incontrovertible evidence of God's acceptance of Cornelius and his household is the gift of the Holy Spirit. This gift, Peter now argues, is given in response to what God sees in people's hearts. That they, circumcised Jews, and now also Cornelius, an uncircumcised Gentile, have received the gift of the Holy Spirit can only mean that God sees no difference between them. Faith is the key to receiving the forgiveness of sins.

Verses 10-11

Peter claims that to demand circumcision of Gentiles who believe is to defy God. He now adds a further argument. The burden of the Law has always been intolerable for the people of Israel. No one has been able to fulfil the demands of the Law, therefore it should not be imposed on others. Relationship with God is established both for Jews and for Gentiles by the gift of God's love made known in Jesus.

To think and talk about:
- How far is it true that to become a Christian today you have to accept not only the Christian Gospel but also church culture?
- Peter began by letting his faith fit in with his cultural world-view. He ended up making his world-view fit in with his faith. What do we take for granted from our world-view that we really ought to challenge?

We have come to the end of our look at Peter, and the significant milestones in his life. His encounter with Jesus led into an incredible journey of faith, which turned his whole world upside-down... but not all at once. As a final exercise, reflect on the changes which took place in Peter's life, as more and more of his lifestyle and personality became shaped by the preacher from Nazareth who had called him from his fishing-nets.

To think and talk about:
● Compare Peter the Galilean fisherman with the Peter of Acts 11 and 15.
How does he see his future?
What are his hopes and dreams?
What are the dangers which face him?
How would his close friends describe him?
What does he value?
Who values him?
Who are his friends?
What differences are there in his lifestyle?
How has his relationship with God changed?
(Members of the group could work in pairs, taking one or two questions each.)

NOTES FOR LEADERS

Bible Exploration is intended as an enjoyable way of helping Explorers to get to know the Bible and to apply it in their own lives. Both this *Guidebook* and the *Workbooks* have been designed as aids rather than as ends in themselves. The purpose is to stimulate discussion and encourage intellectual curiosity among the Explorers, whatever their age. Use the books as a springboard for further work with your group and add other activities which will capture their interest and enthusiasm. Those groups who wish may also sit the final *Question Papers*.

Groups

Leaders should allocate Explorers to a colour group on the basis of their ability as well as their age. This means that a Green group might, for example, consist of children ranging in age from 9 to 14.

As a general guide, the suggested age-groupings for each colour are:

ORANGE	Under 9 years	BLUE	13 and 14 years
YELLOW	9 and 10 years	PURPLE	15 to 17 years
GREEN	11 and 12 years	WHITE	18 years and over

When taking Explorers' ages into consideration, work on the basis of their age at the start of the school year. While there is no lower age-limit for Explorers, the biblical matter selected for the *Bible Exploration* and the questions set assume that no child taking part will be under seven years of age. Leaders who feel that it would be appropriate for younger children to take part may, however, include them.

Organizers' Information Pack

This includes:
- Guidelines for leaders, organizers, assessors and invigilators.
- Hints on assessing *Workbooks*, with answers and suggested marking schemes.
- Additional resources.

This pack may be ordered in the same way as the *Question Papers* (see page 47).

Practical Suggestions

ORANGE, YELLOW, GREEN and BLUE Groups
Throughout the *Guidebook* you will find suggested activities and pointers for discussion designed to help you to relate the biblical material to the Explorers' experience of life and faith. Select those which you feel to be most appropriate to the ages and abilities of the Explorers in your group.

Try to use different methods to explore the material (e.g. quizzes or role-plays) which will help the Explorers to remember the Bible passages.

From time to time, extra Bible verses or passages are referred to in the *Guidebook* and the *Workbooks*. These are intended to help the Explorers in their understanding of the theme. Questions in the *Papers* will be based only on the passages in the syllabus but older Explorers may wish to refer to this additional material in their answers.

Encourage the Explorers to read the passages often and to do a little work each day if they can. Remember, however, that they may be under a lot of pressure with school homework and other activities.

PURPLE and WHITE Groups
The notes on the Bible passages include pointers for discussion and activities to help groups consider the wider issues and apply what they are studying.

Explorers in these groups will want to refer to commentaries and Bible handbooks; these can often be borrowed from ministers or preachers or from the local library.

Some Explorers will be used to sorting out their ideas and expressing them in essay form. Others may need some help and practice in arranging their ideas and putting them down on paper, in which case it may be helpful for them to discuss their ideas with their group leader before writing them down. Practice in composing answers can be very helpful in the final stages of study.

Question Papers

Ordering Question Papers
Question Papers should be ordered using the form on the *Bible Exploration* leaflet or the general order form in the 1997-98 NCEC catalogue, or by writing to NCEC, 1020 Bristol Road, Selly Oak, Birmingham B29 6LB. The *Question Papers* will be available from mid-October 1997.

Sitting the Question Papers
Groups may sit the *Question Papers* at any time of the year as there is no longer a National Competition. It is for the organizers to decide, in consultation with all who are involved in *Bible Exploration* in their church or area, when the Question Papers should be completed and under what conditions.

The time allowed for the *Question Papers* is also at the discretion of the organizers in consultation with group leaders. The following times are intended as a guide only:

ORANGE	45 minutes	BLUE	1 hour 30 minutes
YELLOW	45 minutes	PURPLE	2 hours
GREEN	1 hour	WHITE	2 hours 30 minutes

N.B. In response to comments received these times are no longer printed on the *Question Papers*. Please make sure that all Explorers know how long they have to answer their paper.

Explorers in the PURPLE and WHITE groups are allowed to use their Bibles in answering questions.

The *Question Papers* for ORANGE, YELLOW and GREEN will follow the same format as the Explorers have become used to in their *Workbooks*. They will require knowledge of the Bible passages, and there will be some multiple choice questions. There will be the opportunity for Explorers to illustrate some of their answers. It would be useful therefore for them to be supplied with felt-tipped pens or crayons.

Those answering questions on the BLUE Paper will require deeper understanding of the Bible passages. There will also be the opportunity for some imaginative writing. In order to ease the transition from GREEN, the questions have been designed to be answered in short paragraphs rather than in essay style. Explorers will be expected to answer four questions plus the compulsory question, which will be the last on the paper.

Those answering questions on the PURPLE and WHITE *Question Papers* will be expected to have background knowledge of the passages studied and to relate these to wider issues and to the present day. Explorers will be expected to answer the first question plus four others.